An Artist at
Angkor

An Artist at Angkor

Somboon Phuangdorkmai

With an Introduction by

John Hoskin

Mark Standen
Publishing

*The central complex
of Angkor Wat
(75 x 55 cm).*

*Previous pages:
Banteay Kdei, water-
colour (75 x 55 cm,
detail), sketch of Chau
Say Tevoda.*

Published in 1996 by
Mark Standen Publishing Company Ltd.
43/364 Moo Bahn Amarinnivet 1, Bangkhen
Bangkok 10220, Thailand
Tel: (66 2) 552 4020
Fax: (66 2) 970 6254

Distributed in Cambodia and Vietnam by
Monument Books Ltd.
228 Monivong Street, Phnom Penh
Cambodia
Tel: (855 23) 427154
Fax: (855 23) 426586

ILLUSTRATIONS:
© Somboon Phuangdorkmai 1996
TEXT:
© Mark Standen Publishing
Company Ltd. 1996

ISBN 974 253 001 7

DESIGN
Annie Vaillancourt
Format & Partners Ltd., Bangkok

PHOTO CREDITS
Mark Standen: Pages 10, 40, 108
André Lurde: Page 15

EDITOR
Keith Hardy

REPRODUCTION
Rainbow Graphic Arts Company Ltd.
Hong Kong

PRINTED AND BOUND IN HONG KONG BY
Paramount Printing Company Ltd.

The publisher would like to
thank the companies whose
assistance has made this
book possible:

THAI AIRWAYS
INTERNATIONAL

SHELL COMPANY
OF CAMBODIA AND
SHELL DU LAOS

INDOCHINE INSURANCE
UNION

INDOCHINE RESORTS

*Jungle vegetation
surrounds the evocative
ruins of Ta Prohm
(75 x 55 cm).*

*Overleaf: the stone
causeway leading to
the South Gate of
Angkor Thom.*

Contents

Foreword

The ancient Khmer architects, stonemasons and sculptors who fashioned the majestic monuments of Angkor have recently acquired a modern colleague, Thai artist Somboon Phuangdorkmai. An extremely talented young painter, Khun Somboon has produced a now famous series of watercolours and sketches of the temple ruins. Presented in this book are the finest of her works, sensitive renditions of the fantastic creations of the Kings of Angkor which capture the beauty of ancient forms in a fresh modern style.

Somboon has already shared her art with many people through exhibitions, the success of which has led to this permanent record of her achievement. The paintings and sketches which follow not only portray the grandeur of the ancient Khmer civilization, but also, more importantly, symbolize the shared heritage and the unique relationship which exists between the kingdoms of Thailand and Cambodia.

Those who have already visited Angkor will find in this book memories recalled with the vividness of dreams. Those who have yet to see the monuments will undoubtedly find compelling reasons to go and experience their wonder in person. The form and meaning of these stunning sights humble the mind, lift the spirit and touch the soul. In short, as Khun Somboon's marvellous works richly attest, the magic is still there!

H.E. Roland Eng
**Ambassador Extraordinary and Plenipotentiary
of The Kingdom of Cambodia to The Kingdom of Thailand**

Untouched by archae-
ologists, much of Ta
Prohm remains in the
grip of huge trees
(27 x 37 cm).

Facing page: detail of
stone gateway between
Phimeanakas and the
Elephant Terrace.

Previous pages: left,
the artist at Angkor
and, right, detail
of stone carving at
Ta Som.

An Introduction

There is a popular belief that Angkor was rediscovered in 1860 by French naturalist Henri Mouhot. But although what had been the capital of the ancient Khmer empire was abandoned in the 15th century and left to the ravages of the tropical forest, the city was never lost or forgotten. It remained a site of religious pilgrimage, and its existence was known, in fact or rumour, to a long line of European adventurers and missionaries. What Mouhot did achieve, through his posthumously published travel diaries, was to fire the imagination of a Western audience.

But if Mouhot did not strictly rediscover Angkor — and he never made any such claim for himself — his story does highlight the extraordinary power of the ruins to inspire wonder. Although we know far more facts about Angkor today, we still half want to believe in some miraculous discovery. So vast in extent and so evocative in appearance are the monuments that, in a sense, each of us rediscovers Angkor anew and cannot help but marvel at the sight.

Visiting Angkor Wat in 1962, English writer Sacheverell Sitwell recorded: "This is what we think in the first moment of seeing the five towers rising before our eyes; that some being of Pharaonic importance whose very name has been forgotten lived here, that he reigned here, or came here to be buried… Just the approach to Angkor Wat is on a grander scale than anything in the living world."

Today, Thai artist Somboon Phuangdorkmai, even though familiar with ancient oriental architecture in her own country, responds with similar amazement. She describes her first impressions of Angkor as, "Wow! I was just wide-eyed from the first moment. I was surprised at the vastness of the site and the huge scale of the monuments. How, I wondered, did man manage to build such marvels in stone?" Her amazement was all the greater for Angkor being a totally unexpected experience — she simply had never planned to visit the ruins.

It was while Somboon was in Phnom Penh to open an exhibition in January, 1994, that a friend told the then 34-year-old artist that she ought to make a side trip to Angkor. She took his advice, expecting to spend just two or three days among the ruins before heading back to her studio in Bangkok. But such was the impact of Angkor on the artist's imagination that what was intended as a brief holiday turned into a three-and-a-half-month stay, broken only by two quick trips back to Thailand to replenish stocks of paper and paints. It proved to be a highly productive period yielding more than 100 paintings and three full sketch-books.

"I felt possessed by a desire to capture my feelings," Somboon remarks. "Every day I'd walk and stop and sketch and paint, walk, sketch and paint." The passion Somboon felt for Angkor was reflected in her work, and she painted entirely on location with remarkable speed and complete assurance.

Following a long tradition of travellers who have attempted to capture Angkor on paper — Mouhot had sketched the ruins, as did Louis Delaporte, the official artist attached to the 1860s French Mekong expedition — Somboon became thoroughly immersed in a sense of discovery. The visual impact of the

Above: the artist sketching the North Gate of Angkor Thom.

Facing page: the finished work.

temples, their symbolism, their relation to their surroundings and their testament to man's achievement all enthralled her.

Indeed, it is easy to lose oneself at Angkor, not in the geographical sense, but in terms of being absorbed by the ruins. The monuments are so different in scale and genius to anything subsequently created in Cambodia that they seem to exist outside of time and place. Sixteenth-century Portuguese and Spanish adventurers, the first Europeans to see the ruined temples, could not believe they had been built by the Khmer, and thought they must have been the work of Alexander the Great, or the Romans, or, as local myth would have it, the gods. Even now, Angkor stands so starkly alone, surrounded by forest that constantly threatens to reassert the supremacy of nature over man, that it is easy to imagine mythical rather than historical origins.

Street scene of Siem Reap showing typical French colonial-style architecture (27 x 37 cm).

In spite of appearances, however, Angkor is the product of evolving civilization on the Indochinese peninsula. It had its antecedents, although it was to blossom into something far greater than anything that had ever gone before.

Located close to the modern town of Siem Reap, just beyond the northern shore of the Tonle Sap (Great Lake) in western Cambodia, Angkor derives its name from the Sanskrit *nagara*, meaning 'city', and it was here that a succession of Khmer kings had their capital from which they ruled over an empire that covered not only what is now Cambodia but also large areas of Laos, Thailand and Vietnam. The ruins seen today are not those of a single city, for each king recreated or realigned his capital as he erected monuments to his own reign. But, except for one short period, the area of Angkor remained the power base of the ancient Khmer for six centuries with only the focal point of the city undergoing periodic change.

Classically picturesque, the western section of Preah Kahn is framed by lush vegetation (75 x 55 cm).

The Khmer are first known to have lived along the lower and middle reaches of the Mekong river in what is now northern Cambodia and southern Laos. The broad pattern of early civilization in the area is one of independent petty city states developing in the late centuries BC and the early years of the Christian era. Gradually the strongest of these states conquered or assimilated neighbours to form kingdoms and virtual empires.

While it is clear that indigenous populations gradually developed a distinct and comparatively high degree of civilization in the lower Mekong basin, the rise of large and powerful kingdoms was assisted to a greater or lesser extent by external influences from India. In a process of 'Indianization', much of Southeast Asia adopted or adapted to various political, social and religious concepts that had their roots in ancient India and were transmitted to the region by merchants and other travellers following the sea trade route to China.

Historical facts about Indianization are few, and the precise nature and extent of its influence is a matter of some controversy. Certainly, it was not a question of colonization but of a gradual and selective process whereby local elites, without abandoning their inherited customs and traditions, incorporated elements of Indian culture into their own civilization, thereby fostering conditions for the growth of large unified states.

Angkor was to be the ultimate beneficiary of Indianization in mainland Southeast Asia, but it was preceded by two earlier kingdoms, Funan and Chenla. Centred on the delta coast and lower reaches of the Mekong and inhabited mostly by people belonging to the Mon-Khmer group, Funan was founded in the 1st century AD and flourished until the 5th century, after which it was gradually superseded by Chenla, focused further up the Mekong close to the present Cambodia-Laos border.

The history of both Funan and Chenla is sketchy and relies largely on Chinese chronicles whose accounts, while offering intriguing insights, are fragmentary and unreliable. For example, although the word 'Funan' appears in Chinese texts, it is probably a mispronunciation of *bnam*, 'mountain', and the actual name of the kingdom is unknown. It is also uncertain whether Funan and Chenla were unified states or, as was more likely, simply the largest and most aggressive of a number of loosely allied principalities. What is important is that Funan and Chenla, as Indianized states of considerable political, social, technical and cultural attainment, prepared the ground for the eventual flowering of Angkor as a fully-fledged civilization rooted in Indian culture but assuming its own distinct identity.

The name 'Angkor' refers both to the empire ruled by Khmer kings and to the complex of monumental buildings that marked their capital. The birth of the state preceded the founding of the city, and the date generally given as denoting the start of the Angkorian period is 802, when the Khmer king Jayavarman II consolidated his power and instituted the cult of the *deva raj*, or 'god king'. This originally Indian concept had been adopted by Funan and was later used by the Angkorian monarchs to legitimize power and generate political unity.

Angkor arose out of the collapse of Chenla, whose decline opened the way for the creation of a new political structure. But quite how this came about is uncertain. Possibly, internal conflict had weakened Chenla (there had earlier been a split into two states, 'Water Chenla' and 'Land Chenla'), while external attacks by Java could have contributed to general instability. Yet Jayavarman being denoted as the second monarch of that name suggests a degree of continuity. Nonetheless, something new was taking place. "It would be a mistake to divest the reign of Jayavarman II of all special significance," writes historian Ian Mabbett "The very fact that it was later looked back upon as the beginning of a pan-Khmer regime indicates that there was, however gradually it was consolidated, a real discontinuity between the jostling principalities of Chenla and the empire that came into being during the ninth and tenth centuries."

In addition to pursuing the deva raj cult as a means of consolidating political unity, Jayavarman II initiated an important territorial shift away from

The artist was intrigued by nature's dominance over the ruins of Ta Prohm (27 x 37 cm).

Bustling activity at a fish market on the banks of the Tonle Sap.

the Mekong valley sites of Chenla cities and the earlier coastal settlements of Funan towards a new focus north of the Tonle Sap. In a reign involving almost ceaseless travel, Jayavarman II repeatedly moved his power base, finally settling at Hariharalaya (the present-day village of Roluos). He did not found Angkor itself, which lies a few kilometres northwest of his last capital, but he had effectively created a new centre for the Khmer world.

The Khmer state was essentially agrarian (although trade did contribute significantly to the Angkorian economy), and by relocating close to the Tonle Sap Jayavarman II secured an invaluable natural advantage. The annual flooding of the lake produced intensely fertile land suited to wet rice cultivation, while the waters supported a teeming fish population. Angkor was thus ensured of a plentiful food supply which, in an agrarian age, was the basis of power. Moreover, transport and

trade were also served by the lake which, connected to the Mekong via the Tonle Sap river, offered a communication link to the outside world.

Jayavarman II's two immediate successors remained at Hariharalaya, but Yasovarman I (r.889–900) moved his capital a little way northwest and founded Yasodharapura, the first city of Angkor, with its centre at Phnom Bakheng. This natural hill gave Yasovarman the ideal site on which to build a temple that would be representative of Mount Meru, the mountain of the gods in Hindu cosmology.

Apart from a brief interval when the court moved to Koh Ker (921–944), some 100 kilometres northeast of Angkor, the area was to remain the site of the capital for the next four centuries, and a pattern was set upon which future monarchs would elaborate. As the king was deemed to be a god on earth, so his capital city should symbolize the universe in miniature, with Mount Meru at its centre.

Sunset over the Western Baray dramatically captured in a view from Phnom Bakheng (37 x 27 cm).

*Western Mebon
sketched from the
banks of the Western
Baray in which it
stands on a circular
island.*

Thus the temple mountain came to form the core of city planning at Angkor, each king erecting his own increasingly complex architectural representation of the cosmos which, on his death, became his funerary monument. Yasovarman I had built his temple mountain on a hill, but a natural eminence was not essential to the architecture and later shrines were erected on level ground with Mount Meru symbolized in the tiered terraces of pyramid temples.

Symbolism was central to Khmer art and architecture, most emphatically expressed in the temple mountain, and this accounts in large measure for the awe-inspiring effect that Angkor's enduring monuments continue to exert. As Ian Mabbett comments, "Each building was imitating the ideal form in heaven in order to realize it on earth… If the institutions of Khmer political unity were to persist, people needed a vocabulary to describe it, a set of terms that would give the king a role transcending the traditions of locality and making of his kingdom an image of a transcendent city of the gods. Hence the obsessive cosmological symbolism that made nearly every detail of metropolitan art an evocation of the divine."

Angkor's urban genius was not limited to its stone monuments; water also played a crucial role in civic organization. Employing sophisticated engineering techniques the Angkorian kings built a huge network of reservoirs (*barays*), pools, canals and moats in an hydraulic system that equalled the scale and complexity of their architectural achievements. Water management had been a feature of Funan but it was raised to a new dimension at Angkor, first by Yasovarman I who constructed the Eastern Baray, measuring seven by two kilometres and with an estimated capacity of 60 million cubic metres. Later, in the 11th century, even this huge reservoir was surpassed by the Western Baray which measured eight by two kilometres and had a probable maximum capacity of 70 million cubic metres.

The precise purpose of Angkor's hydraulic system is, however, a matter of debate among historians. It was earlier generally assumed that water management was constructed to control the annual floods, draining water in the wet season and providing irrigation during the dry months, hence guaranteeing a vast agricultural output. Others now argue that irrigation was not extensively employed, and the reservoirs served more a ritual rather than a practical purpose, being part of the city's cosmological symbolism. The question has still to be resolved, although whatever the true function of the hydraulic system, it bears testament to the brilliance of Angkor and serves to define the city in a way equal if different to that of the temple mountains.

In addition to being a most remarkable builder and hydraulic engineer, Yasovarman I was also a formidable warrior and during his reign Angkor began to emerge as a true empire, eventually holding sway over lands that possibly extended as far north as the border of China, south to the upper part of the

A timeless scene of rural activity, scooping water to irrigate the rice crop.

Malay peninsula, east to Champa (in present-day southern Vietnam) and west into what is now Thailand. A score of kings succeeded Yasovarman I over the next 300 years, during which time Angkor remained the dominant political and cultural force in the region, suffering only a temporary reversal at the hands of the Cham in 1177. Succession was not always smooth and internal conflicts weakened the state from time to time, but a number of extraordinarily accomplished monarchs preserved Angkor's hegemony while adding to the city's architectural glory.

Two reigns in particular stand out. Under Suryavarman II (r.1113-1150) Angkor entered its Golden Age, both politically and culturally. The empire was at its peak, while the capital city boasted a hydraulic system unmatched in the region, and a complex of gilded temples that attested to the wealth, piety and authority of the monarchy. Most emphatically, Suryavarman II was the builder of Angkor Wat, the chief masterpiece of Khmer architecture, which survives today as the most famous monument to Angkor's glory.

Facing page: the artist first studied Angkor Wat through pen drawings before attempting any paintings.

The largest of the temple mountains, Angkor Wat is surrounded by a moat 180 metres wide and has an outer enclosure measuring 815 metres by 1,000 metres. Beyond a second enclosure a central pyramid rises over three terraces, each surrounded by cloisters and galleries, and is topped by five towers, the tallest standing 65 metres above ground level. Adding beauty to the awesome proportions is a mass of decorative detail. Vanished is the gilt that once covered the temple, but there remain the exquisite bas-relief carvings which cover virtually every flat surface and depict scenes from epic legends, wars and courtly life, as well as figures of *apsaras* (celestial dancers) of which there are some 2,000 throughout the temple complex.

Angkor entered a troubled period after the reign of Suryavarman II but fortunes were brilliantly restored by Jayavarman VII (r.1181–c.1218). A man of outstanding ability, he not only defeated the Cham who had earlier taken Angkor, but also embarked on an empire-wide reconstruction and expansion programme. He also built the last city at Angkor, Angkor Thom, which is centred on the enigmatic Bayon temple mountain.

Jayavarman VII was the last of the great builder-kings and Angkor's glory waned after his death. Although the empire continued to be powerful and prosperous for another two centuries, a slow but steady decline set in. Increasingly, the Khmer were threatened by the Thai to the west who, in 1431, succeeded in sacking Angkor. The Khmer then abandoned the city and while they re-established themselves on the banks of the Mekong near present-day Phnom Penh, they were never again to be the dominant force in the region.

Exactly why Angkor was deserted is unclear. The Thai were certainly a threat, but they showed no intention of permanent occupation. Probably, a combination of factors led to the demise of the city — agricultural failure, adverse effects of deforestation, a population weakened by wars and possibly a malaria epidemic could all have contributed to the decline. In broader regional terms, the 15th century was the beginning of an age of commerce which favoured coastal powers, not Angkor's inland agrarian state. It is significant to note that the Thai capital of Ayutthaya, in many ways Angkor's cultural heir, derived strength from its outlet to the sea via the Chao Phraya river.

If the power and influence of Cambodia today fails to echo even faintly the past, the cultural legacy of Angkor is enormous. The architectural achievement of

The artist's first painting of the Bayon, a temple she found especially intriguing (75 x 55 cm).

the Khmer was never equalled by any other mainland Southeast Asian culture. As one commentator has aptly noted, "The Khmers left the world no systems of administration, education or ethics like those of the Chinese; no literatures, religions or systems of philosophy like those of India; but here [at Angkor] oriental architecture and decoration reached its culminating point."

Angkor's temple architecture has immediate impact, and although inherently symbolic in function, its power and originality can be appreciated without explanations. Unlike, for example, Christian cathedrals, temple mountains were not designed to enclose a vast space — they were required to house a god, not a

The late 9th-century Preah Koh temple at Roluos, southeast of the main Angkor complex (37 x 27 cm).

congregation. Consequently they are elaborate masses intended to impress the viewer from afar, and follow the principle, also found in ancient Greek architecture, that the majestic aspect of a monument is most apparent when viewed from a distance of twice its greatest dimension.

Stylistically, Angkor's architectural roots are planted in the Indian temples of the Gupta period (4th-6th centuries AD) which, although subject to elaboration and duplication of forms, took as their basic structure a rectangular enclosed space topped by multiple stepped stone roofs and adorned with relief carving.

From this model the Khmer evolved their own distinctive temple architecture. The earliest pre-Angkor prototypes were most likely constructed in wood, while later building progressively used brick, laterite and, ultimately, sandstone from which Angkor's greatest masterpieces were constructed.

As Ian Mabbett and others have pointed out, the temples of Angkor follow two basic patterns. One is that of a collection of tower sanctuaries dedicated to a group of deities, and the other is a central sanctuary raised on a square pyramid and dedicated to a patron god, most often Siva but there are exceptions, notably it is Vishnu who is honoured at Angkor Wat. An example of the first temple type is Preah Koh, dedicated in 879, although the largest and most impressive monuments follow the second pattern which became increasingly elaborate and complex with the addition of walls, galleries and subordinate tower shrines, the form culminating in the scale and complexity of Angkor Wat.

An undoubted masterpiece, impressive not only for its size but also for the perfection of its architecture and relief carvings, Angkor Wat is nonetheless but one of numerous monuments that survive as testament to the achievement of the ancient Khmer at Angkor. One of the world's largest historical sites, the core area of the city (or, more accurately, cities) as seen today is spread over some 200 square kilometres and encompasses more than 70 major monuments.

Smaller than Angkor Wat, but almost as impressive for its haunting appearance, is the Bayon which stands at the centre of Jayavarman VII's city, Angkor Thom. An imposing stone pile of 54 towers, each hauntingly carved with four enigmatic faces of the Bodhisattva Avalokitesvara, it is exceptional for its unique architecture and for the fact that it was dedicated as a Buddhist shrine.

Among other principal sights are the Baphuon, a self-assured looking pyramidal representation of Mount Meru; Preah Kahn, a temple complex of labyrinthine proportions; Ta Prohm, left untouched intentionally by archaeologists and dramatically caught in the grip of jungle vegetation; and, not least, tiny 10th-century Banteay Srei, an architectural gem in red sandstone, standing alone some 30 kilometres from the main temple complex.

While individual monuments are wonders in themselves, perhaps the most remarkable fact about Angkor is that it survives at all. Given the potential of time, climate, monsoon rains and untamed tropical vegetation to wreak damage, the temple ruins are comparatively well preserved. The most important monuments were well restored earlier this century by the French, who first established an Angkor Conservancy in 1908 and maintained an archaeological presence at the site until forced out by civil war in 1972. During Cambodia's recent troubled past Angkor suffered neglect but virtually no actual war damage. Wholesale theft of statuary, however, has been a serious problem.

Several countries and international organizations are currently supporting restoration projects at various temples, and although preservation is an ongoing concern, the general state of the monuments is better than could be reasonably expected considering Cambodia's tragic history.

Although the Khmer never managed to regain the glory that was Angkor, its achievement remains a potent symbol of a heritage that unites the people and the land. So great was that achievement that Angkor today has become in effect a shared world heritage, a testament to the possibilities of man's creativity. It is this which immediately struck a chord with artist Somboon Phuangdorkmai, and

Trees and their shadows frame a side view of Angkor Wat (75 x 55 cm).

impelled her to produce a series of watercolours and sketches which must stand as the fullest painterly attention the monuments have received in recent years.

All visitors to Angkor are tempted to try to capture the glories of the ruins in snapshots, but this is not Somboon's way. "I always carry painting materials with me," she says. "Brushes, paints, pen and paper help to keep my memory sharp. I love travelling but I'm not good at taking photographs, so these items serve as my camera." Although usually so well prepared to practise her art, Somboon was to find Angkor a greater inspiration and a greater challenge than she had ever encountered before.

*A Khmer woman
pedals a bicycle laden
with roofing thatch
(75 x 27 cm, detail).*

Her first studies were of the ruins of Angkor Thom and, although intrigued by the more famous Angkor Wat, it was some time before she found a way to capture the largest of the temple complexes. "At first I could not draw it, it was very hard for me to paint," she explains. "The forms weren't straight or balanced, and it covered such a huge area. I couldn't find the angle I wanted." It wasn't until Somboon ran for shelter from a rain storm that she accidentally saw the perspective she was seeking. After that serendipitous discovery Angkor Wat became an obsession and the artist would stop there "every day, even after painting more distant sites. It became like a ritual… Every detail, every stone was steeped in beauty."

As a Thai and an artist, Somboon also made personal discoveries, realizing for the first time the full extent of the cultural heritage Thailand had absorbed from the ancient Khmer. In the decorative detail of the temples, for example, she saw the original forms of the traditional designs and motifs she had been taught as an art student. She even noted a similarity between the Khmer and archaic Thai words for 'artist'.

It is this idea of discovery which perhaps accounts for the freshness of her paintings. Covering virtually all of Angkor's major temple complexes, from the massive and majestic Angkor Wat to the tiny sandstone jewel of Banteay Srei, the works are impressionistic and evocative. Light colours verging on monochrome and rapid brushwork give the effect of transcending the mass of the stone, allowing viewers to see the ruins for themselves rather than be confronted with a simple likeness. "I want people to share the same experience I had, the same sense of discovery," Somboon remarks.

The sketches, which include scenes of contemporary Cambodian daily life as well as the temples, are similarly evocative, and the works as a whole derive power from their directness. Nothing is contrived. "My paintings and drawings show what I saw and how I felt," Somboon says. "Before I started painting or drawing, I didn't think about overall concepts. I just began to work when I found scenes and subjects I liked."

Immediacy and a sure confidence in what she does underpins all Somboon's work, which covers a surprising range. Whereas most other Thai artists are content to paint in one style, often to the point of repetition, Somboon positively revels in versatility. The watercolours of Angkor stand in marked contrast to the artist's earlier surrealistic oils dealing with social issues, especially the suffering of women and children. Different again are vibrant landscapes and floral studies, or the fragmented almost Braque-like statements which were inspired by a 1995 visit to France, at the time in the throes of labour protests.

It is this range which makes Somboon such an exciting talent and sets her apart in the contemporary art scene as one of Thailand's most innovative artists, challenging forms, media and norms. The variety of her works transcends mere technique — although oils and watercolours tend to be used alternately to reflect respectively darker and lighter moods — and her expressive power embraces equally a celebration of life and a critique of its injustices. There is, however, a common, unifying factor in Somboon's sketching, which holds a key to a full appreciation of her art.

"You can tell a real artist from his or her sketches," remarks Atsuko Suzuki Davies, Somboon's close friend and manager. "Picasso was an incredible

A good luck charm swings from the rear-view mirror in one of the artist's Bangkok taxi sketch studies.

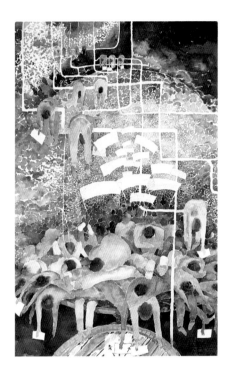

*"Tired from Work"
inspired by a 1995
French labour strike,
watercolour
(55 x 115 cm).*

sketcher, that's why his abstracts are so outstanding. Sketches form the basis of all paintings and Somboon has that rare skill."

Somboon is a compulsive sketcher, pulling out her pad and pen in planes, cars, trains, wherever she happens to be and something catches her eye. In a matter of minutes her fluid line captures a momentary scene, a fleeting impression, a telling pose. Scattered around her studio are scores of sketch-books full of drawings, some intended as finished works, others merely visual jottings of ideas to be later developed in full-scale paintings.

As David Hockney once said, "Learning to draw is learning to look." Somboon is not a self-taught artist, but she appears driven to learn, to look and ultimately to translate what she sees and feels into paintings which constantly take her in new directions.

"I try to draw every day," Somboon remarks as she displays sketch-books covering virtually every phase of her career to date and every form from nude figure studies to the jumble of garlands and trinkets hanging from the rear-view mirrors of taxi-cabs. The earliest sketches are figure studies done while attending short drawing courses during travels in Europe. At first the line is tentative, but gradually greater assurance is apparent as the artist develops the fluid style that characterizes her best sketches, where an almost continuous, weaving line captures outlines with striking accuracy.

The skill developed in making rapid, sure sketches translates into the paintings both thematically, in the "seeing", and technically, inasmuch as works are executed swiftly and, usually, directly from the artist's visual experience. All this is considerably removed from what is conventionally taught Thai art students, who are commonly drilled into taking time and painstaking care at the expense of losing immediacy.

The directness and spontaneity of the sketches parallels Somboon's whole approach to her art. It is something she feels she has to do, but also loves to do. "Most Thai artists think they have to learn only one style, as if to say 'this is me', and they are afraid that if they change their style people will not recognize them," Somboon comments. "For me, I feel happy working in all styles. I don't think about selling, about the audience. At first I'm just happy to work and do good painting. I want to be good."

Born into a poor family in Prachinburi province, one of the artist's earliest memories is of drawing and cutting out paper dolls because her parents couldn't afford to buy her proper toys. At school she quickly developed a budding talent, teaching her ^by copying pictures from books, making grid outlines and reproducing paintings square by square. However, in spite of topping her class in art, Somboon was not encouraged in pursuing her studies. Her mother, struggling against poverty and a wayward husband to raise five children, expected her eldest to assist in supporting the family, to find a steady job that would provide a release from daily hardship.

Determined to pursue her art, Somboon felt reluctantly compelled to disappoint her mother, and at sixteen years of age moved to Bangkok with the intention of putting herself through art school. Studying first at the private college of Thaivichitsilp and later at Poh Chang College of Arts and Crafts, the artist was driven by an urge to prove to her mother that there was a career to be made out of painting.

Sketch of a Buddhist monk.

"Who Builds Does Not Live There" depicts the plight of Bangkok construction workers, oil on paper (79 x 106 cm).

Although fulfilling early promise as a student, Somboon failed to win admission to Silpakorn University, Thailand's premier academy of art. Instead, seven years of teaching at Thaivichitsilp followed graduation from Poh Chang, in 1981, before the artist was sufficiently established to support herself by her painting alone.

But missing out on Silpakorn might have been a blessing in disguise as Somboon avoided the ever-present danger of being straightjacketed by academia. Proving to be of greater value was marriage to an employee of an international airline, which afforded the opportunity to travel. The couple were later to divorce, but not before Somboon had toured extensively in Europe, visiting galleries, attending casual art classes and, as always, sketching.

At the same time as pursuing her own art, Somboon has also sought to help and promote other artists through the Roung Pung ('Beehive') Art Community which she helped establish in the 1980s at Bangkok's Weekend Market. Her idea was to create an open-air gallery and meeting place where all artists — writers and musicians as well as painters — could discuss and display their work. Although today she is herself well established, Somboon continues to support Roung Pung as a showcase for lesser-known artists.

While Somboon put in years of hard work before winning the financial success she now enjoys, she quickly achieved critical acclaim. At the start of the 1980s, she formed part of the Vane Group, the first Thai contemporary art collective to expose social injustice through its works. Somboon's paintings had immediate impact — "the most outstanding of the Group," said Alfred Pawlin who, in 1983, hosted the 4th Vane Group Exhibition at his well-known Visual

Dhamma gallery in Bangkok. Subsequently, the artist has exhibited regularly in Bangkok and overseas, in Denmark, Belgium, Japan and Cambodia.

The first painting Somboon ever sold, when she was still a student, was a watercolour, but early in her career she turned increasingly to oils to explore the darker side of life. She never abandoned sketching or watercolours, but her most powerful works of the 1980s and early '90s are largely monochromatic oils of haunting visions. A typical painting of this period, titled simply *Mother*, shows an emaciated naked woman seated beside a dead baby and surrounded by other mutilated human forms. Executed in sepia tones, the picture is totally mute and passive, with attention focused on the woman's staring, accusing eyes.

The picture is actually a portrait of Somboon's mother, and the artist admits to drawing on personal experience, the suffering of her family and her own sadness as a child, for narrative content. But ultimately the works transcend the autobiographical. "My feelings come from my childhood and I need to get these out of my system," Somboon says. "But that is just the starting point. Others suffer, too, and I want people to look at my paintings and think about social issues, about the problems women and children face."

Sad, staring eyes, mouths forming silent screams and agonized human forms are recurring motifs in these paintings which fall loosely into the surrealist mould. "Surrealism was one of the styles we had to study at art school," Somboon explains, "and I was particularly impressed by Salvador Dali; you can see so many things in his pictures. That is what I like about surrealism; it allows you do so much in one picture, and it gives you greater freedom to release inner feelings."

Suffering is given powerful expression in the semi-autobiographical "Mother", oil on paper (79 x 106 cm).

"Golden Shower",
watercolour
(27 x 37 cm).

In visual terms, though, Dali is not the most direct parallel and Somboon's oils bear a closer resemblance to the tormented scenes of Hieronymus Bosch. But influences are largely irrelevant, and the paintings have their own distinct style and expressive force. Oddly, given the frightening and frightful images, the works have a poetic quality in their controlled and honest handling of what are clearly deeply felt emotions.

There is an inescapable passion and intensity about both the artist and her art. Somboon speaks with obvious enthusiasm about her work and the life that informs it, her large eyes, beneath a mop of long unruly hair, as expressive as her voice. "I love these paintings so much," she says of her oils, "that I cannot bring myself to sell them. If I sell them, then only one or two people will see them, but if I keep them, anyone can come and view them at my studio."

Watercolours, on the other hand, Somboon considers her most saleable work, her stock-in-trade. Yet a passion equal if very different to that of her oil paintings has gone into her series of works on Angkor. This is perhaps what finally unifies Somboon's various styles and media — an impassioned immediacy that springs from an uncompromising attempt to portray what she sees, whether literally or with the mind's eye. Nothing is preconceived and the artist is wide-eyed to all around her, never more so than in her discovery of the splendour of Angkor.

"My Life", a semi-abstract self-portrait, watercolour (55 x 115 cm).

Watercolours & Sketches

Encroachment of
nature at Ta Prohm.

Facing page: the
artist surrounded by
curious youngsters
amid the ruins.

*Above: study of lotus
in the moat of Angkor
Wat (75 x 55 cm).*

*Right: gathering lotus
(37 x 27 cm).*

*Previous spread:
sunset over the west
entrance of Angkor
Wat (75 x 55 cm).*

ANGKOR VAT វវ្តអង្គរ
19/1/32

Pen sketch of Angkor Wat viewed from the northwest corner of the temple compound.

Left: majestic Angkor Wat from the artist's favourite perspective (75 x 55 cm).

Sketch of a young Khmer woman in front of the temple.

*Facing page: view of
Angkor Wat from the
southwest (75 x 55 cm).*

*Below: a quick sketch
captures a festive
crowd at Angkor Wat.*

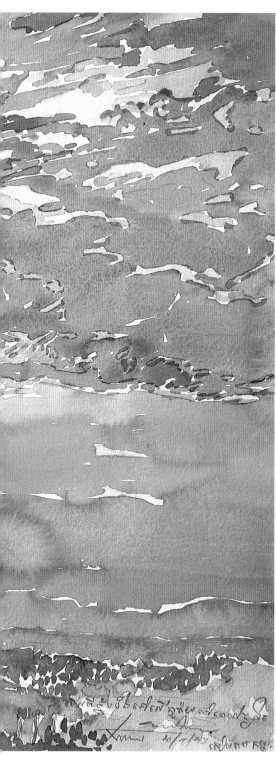

*Sunset over the
Western Baray
treated in watercolour
(37 x 27 cm) and pen
sketch.*

Facing page: the North Gate of Angkor Thom (27 x 37 cm).

Below: sketch of the causeway at the South Gate.

The Bayon, with workers cycling home.

Facing page: the Bayon in closer perspective (75 x 55 cm).

Previous pages: left, falling leaves at Angkor Thom's North Gate (55 cm x 75 cm) and, right, at Preah Kahn (55 x 75 cm).

Studies of the Bayon,
watercolour (75 x 55 cm)
and sketch.

*Right: the impressive
Baphuon pyramid
temple viewed through
foliage (37 x 27 cm).*

*Below: sketch of the
formal approach to
the Baphuon.*

*View of the Elephant
Terrace (75 x 55 cm).*

*Detail of a staircase at
the Elephant Terrace
(37 x 27 cm).*

*Phimeanakas in sketch
study and in water-
colour (37 x 27 cm).*

*Thommanon pictured
in the April hot sea-
son with strong light
and deep shadows
(37 x 27 cm).*

*Previous pages:
individual studies of
the 12 towers of
Prasat Suor Prat
(each 13 x 18 cm).*

Sketch of Thommanon.

*Chau Say Tevoda
(37 x 27 cm).*

Above: the artist's
first painting of Ta
Keo (37 x 27 cm).

Left: later study of
Ta Keo (75 x 55 cm).

Two studies of Ta Prohm: below (37 x 27 cm), and facing page (55 x 75 cm).

General view of Srah
Srang lake (37 x 27 cm).

*Lion statues at Srah
Srang landing terrace
(37 x 27 cm).*

*Left: a ruined tower at
Banteay Kdei
(37 x 27 cm, detail).*

*Far left: Banteay
Kdei viewed from
the eastern approach
(37 x 27 cm).*

Left: thick foliage amongst the ruins of Banteay Kdei (37 x 27 cm).

Below: sketch study of the temple.

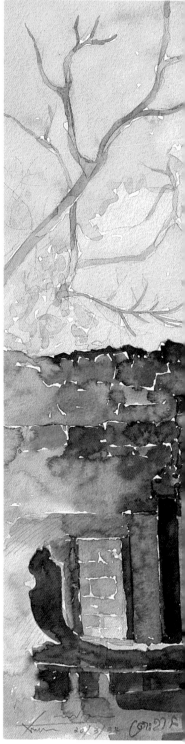

*Preah Kahn: below
(37 x 27 cm), and previ-
ous pages, left (55 x 75
cm), right (37 x 27 cm).*

*Overcast skies create
a surreal atmosphere
at Preah Kahn
(37 x 27 cm).*

*Sketch of a small
chedi at the core
of Preah Kahn.*

*Far left: the temple
in its jungle setting
(75 x 55 cm).*

Sketch of a worker on the path to Neak Pean.

Far right: the island temple of Neak Pean (37 x 27 cm).

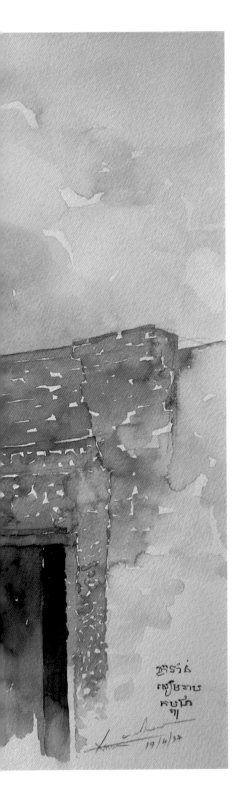

Above: Prasat Kravan
(37 x 27 cm).

Left: brick detail of
Prasat Kravan
(37 x 27 cm).

The brick temple of
Pre Rup (37 x 27 cm).

The island temple of
Eastern Mebon
(37 x 27 cm).

*Studies of the Bakong
at Roluos in sketch
and watercolour
(37 x 27 cm).*

*The eastern approach
at Banteay Srei
(37 x 27 cm).*

*The island temple of
Eastern Mebon
(37 x 27 cm).*

*Studies of the Bakong
at Roluos in sketch
and watercolour
(37 x 27 cm).*

The eastern approach
at Banteay Srei
(37 x 27 cm).

The beautiful red sand-stone temple of Banteay Srei (37 x 27 cm).

*Right: fruit sellers at
Siem Reap market
(37 x 27 cm).*

*Sketch of a Buddhist
shrine close to the
Bayon.*

Impressions of Siem Reap. Left: a vegetable garden (37 x 27 cm). Below: a waterwheel, characteristic of the Siem Reap river.

*Typical rural scenes in
the vicinity of Siem Reap
(both 36 x 28 cm).*

Sketch studies of fisher folk on the shore of the Tonle Sap.

Far right: a picturesque scenic view overlooking the Tonle Sap (37 x 27 cm).

*Somboon Phuangdorkmai
at her studio in Bangkok.*

*Facing page: sketch of the
Eiffel Tower, Paris.*

*Overleaf: trees sprouting
from the ruins of Ta Prohm
(27 x 37 cm).*

Artist's Profile

Education

| 1976-1978 | Thaivichitsilp Art College, Bangkok, Thailand |
| 1979-1981 | Poh Chang College of Arts and Crafts, Bangkok, Thailand |

Exhibitions

1978	1st Vane Group Exhibition, Rajburi, Thailand
1981	Poh Chang College Art Exhibition, Bangkok, Thailand
1982-1983	3rd and 4th Vane Group Exhibitions, Bangkok, Thailand
1984	Silpa Bhirasri Arts Festival, Bangkok, Thailand
	The Ta-Wan Group Exhibition, Bangkok, Thailand
1985	Exhibition, 25th Anniversary of Goethe Institute, Bangkok, Thailand
1986	1st International Women in Art Exhibition, Bangkok, Thailand
	Art for Peace, Bangkok, Thailand
1987	Three Women on Show, Bangkok, Thailand
	International Women Art Exhibition, Bangkok, Thailand
	Art Exhibition for the October Commemoration, Bangkok, Thailand
	An Exhibition of Paintings and Wood Sculptures, Bangkok, Thailand
	Exhibition of Aesthetics in Honour of The King, Bangkok, Thailand
1988	Solo Exhibition, Ostbirk, Denmark
1988-1989	Exhibitions, Roung Pung Art Community, Bangkok, Thailand

1989	Solo Exhibition, Kvindegalleriet, Aarhus, Denmark
	Solo Exhibition: Changing Colours and Emotions, Bangkok, Thailand
1990	Exhibition, Montien Hotel, Bangkok, Thailand
1991	Exhibition, Roung Pung Art Community, Bangkok, Thailand
	Thai-Japanese Women Paintings, Bangkok, Thailand
1992	3rd Annual Bangkok Arts Group Exhibition, Bangkok, Thailand
	2nd International Women in Art Exhibition, Bangkok, Thailand
	Watercolour Painting Exhibition, The Gallery, Bangkok, Thailand
	Solo Exhibition: Landscape, Bangkok, Thailand
	Ratchdamnoen Memory, Bangkok, Thailand
	Exhibition of Works by 21 Thai Women Artists, Bangkok, Thailand
	Asian Young Artists' Exhibition, Tokyo, Japan
1993	Solo Exhibition, Royal Park Travelodge Resort, Phuket, Thailand
	Solo Exhibition, Kinokuniya Bookstore, Bangkok, Thailand
	The Beaten Earth Art Exhibition, Bangkok, Thailand
1993-1994	The Art of Swing Exhibitions I and II, Bangkok, Thailand
1994	Solo Opening Showcase, New Art Gallery, Phnom Penh, Cambodia
	Watercolour Festival, Montien Hotel, Bangkok, Thailand
1995	Solo Exhibition: An Artist at Angkor
	May: The Royal Cambodian Embassy, Bangkok, Thailand
	Sep: The Imperial Queen's Park Hotel, Bangkok, Thailand
	Oct: Akko Collectors' House, Bangkok, Thailand
	Thaise-Vlaansevriendenkring Exhibition, Kookelaere, Belgium
1995-1996'	31st and 32nd Asia Modern Art Exhibitions, Japan
1996'	Solo Exhibition: Taxi Drivers (Pen Sketches), Bangkok, Thailand

Thai Airways International Public Company Ltd., the national flag carrier of the Kingdom of Thailand, began modestly in 1960 as a regional airline serving just ten destinations with three propeller-driven aircraft. Today, it operates a totally modern fleet of 73 aircraft serving 72 destinations in 37 countries across four continents. THAI was the first all-jet airline in Asia. It serves more countries in Asia than any other carrier. With over 20,000 dedicated and experienced staff, THAI is perfectly equipped to provide a service that is as smooth as silk. Currently, over 500,000 members benefit from the airline's own frequent-flyer programme, *Royal Orchid Plus*. THAI remains committed to providing total quality and complete services to all its passengers.

The Royal Dutch/Shell Group of Companies is engaged in various activities relating to oil, natural gas, coal, chemicals and other businesses, making it one of the world's largest enterprises. Shell's involvement with Cambodia dates back to the 1920s. In 1992, after an absence of 17 years, Shell became one of the first foreign companies to return to Cambodia to invest and contribute to its reconstruction and development. Today, the Shell Company of Cambodia is the largest multinational oil company in Cambodia. With its fuel depot in Sihanouk-ville, aviation depot in Pochentong, expanding network of retail stations, and investments in facilities and human resources, Shell is affirming its current and long-term commitment to the growth and development of Cambodia.

Since its creation in 1993, **Indochine Insurance Union** has become the largest general insurance operation in Cambodia. The Company has a major share of insurance of aid or rehabilitation projects, as well as multinational corporations. With good penetration into the emerging purely Cambodian market, and a growing number of national branch offices, Indochine Insurance Union illustrates perfectly the growth potential of the Cambodian economy.

Jersey-based **Indochine Resorts** is a property development company focusing specifically on superior tourism facilities in Indochina. The Company's first such facility in Cambodia, situated at Siem Reap, is a hotel complex (opening November 1997). Complementing most sensitively the unique beauty of Angkor, the hotel is perfect for the discerning traveller drawn by the compelling sense of intellectual adventure waiting to be experienced in the ancient Khmer capital.

Acknowledgements

The artist would like to thank the following people whose kind advice
and generous assistance has helped in so many ways:

His Excellency Roland Eng, Ed Fitzgerald,

Atsuko Suzuki Davies, Dédé Lurde, Mark Standen,

John Hoskin, Keith Hardy, Annie Vaillancourt
and, not least, the people of Siem Reap
for their warm hospitality.